BEST SELLER STRATEGIES

CASH OUT PRONTO

BRENTON FERNANDEZ

It matters who you work with to
sell your most valuable investment!

Cash Out Pronto

ISBN: 978-0-692-68305-7

Printed in the United States of America

Cover designer:
Apricot Studio
Apricot.studio

Book Editor:
Tisha Marie Enterprises

Interior Formatter:
One To One Creative Services
OneToOneCreative.com

INTRODUCTION

Your home is likely your single largest asset, deciding to sell it is a big decision — perhaps the biggest financial one of your life. If you are thinking about selling your home, this guide will save you tons of time, aggravation and keep a lot more money in your pocket. I've strived to keep this guide as short as possible and be considerate of your time, while still conveying a full and detailed breadth of knowledge.

Most homeowners decide to sell about once every six to nine years. In that same amount of time, I have the privilege of assisting many families with listing and selling their home.

In this guide we will take a detailed look at the following:

1. In chapter 1, we will examine the emotional process involved in selling and how to prepare yourself.
2. In chapters 2–4, we will look at the three most important factors to getting your home SOLD!
3. In chapters 5–8, we will look at how to hire the right agent, handle showings, work with offers and get your home successfully closed and SOLD!

If you have any real estate related questions or wish to set up a free, no obligation consultation, please do not hesitate to contact me.

To Your Success!

CONTENTS

① DECIDING TO SELL

It goes without saying that the first step in the home selling process is making the decision to sell. For some, this decision will be difficult and emotional. For others, the decision will come quite readily. There are a plethora of reasons that spark the idea of selling in a homeowner's mind. However, what I've found in my practice is that by the time a homeowner contacts me to sell their home; they have already made the decision to sell; provided they can achieve their goals through the selling process.

One thing is absolutely certain. If you are considering moving, you are not alone! According to the U.S. Census Bureau, since the 1990s more than 40 million Americans a year decide to move. What's more, approximately one third of these folks move across the county or state line. According to a recent study by moving giant Bekin, 70 percent of all residential moves are within the same county. In our area, thousands of sellers successfully SOLD their home last year alone. This number has been fairly consistent for several years.

MAKING THE DECISION

According to Inman News, the three most common reasons for selling are 1) family-related, 2) work-related, and 3) housing-related. If a homeowner receives a job transfer, gets a new job or simply finds the daily commute unbearable, he/she will often make the decision to sell and purchase a property closer to his or her workplace. Other common reasons for relocating include 1) being closer to church or family, 2) the desire to live in a different city or a better part of town, 3) better home amenities, 4) a growing (or shrinking) family, 5) personal hardship, 6) getting the kids into a better school system or 7) simply the desire to upsize or downsize.

Top 10 Reasons People Move

1. New or better home
2. Moving out on their own
3. More affordable housing
4. New job or employee relocation
5. Moving closer to work
6. Lower crime rate
7. Wanted to buy a home (for those renting)
8. Loss of employment
9. Better weather
10. Due to natural disaster

(Source: Bekin Moving 2011 report)

For those facing a hardship, the most common include:

1. Loss of income
2. Increased expenses
3. Medical problems
4. Divorce/absolved relationship
5. Death in the family

EMOTIONAL CHALLENGES

In my real estate practice, I have observed that most homeowners greatly underestimate the emotional challenges involved in the selling process, especially if you are selling out of need versus desire. In fact, compared to buying a home, selling can be a downright emotionally draining process. For those selling out of necessity or hardship, the emotional toll can be even greater.

The emotional challenges to selling are many. First you have to get your home ready to sell. Doing small fixes that you never got around to and spending money on a home you will no longer own can be a drag. Then you have to deal with the whole selling process — working with an agent, setting the price, having your home 'show-ready' at all times, negotiating the sale, etc. And to top it all off, you still have to pack up your entire house and relocate your family. Whew! Having second thoughts?

I firmly believe that in order for you to avoid disappointment during the selling process, we must set the right expectations. Just like an athlete preparing for a marathon, you must be mentally prepared for the challenges that lie ahead. Selling your home is a life event. Trust me. By preparing yourself mentally, you will arrive on the other side a much better person.

My real estate practice is big on using the right systems and partnering with the right people. Therefore, my job is to make my client's journey through the selling process as painless and stress-free as possible.

My number one job is to educate my clients.

Over the years, I have come to realize that most folks are sane and rational. Thus, if I can provide them with the right information, they can make the right decisions for their family. Therefore, I don't spend time trying to convince my clients to sell. When armed with the right information, my clients know whether it is in their best interest to sell now, wait, or in some cases, to abandon the idea of selling completely.

For me, it is always most helpful to understand my client's motivation for selling, and to educate them on the selling process (what I do to successfully sell homes), and let them make an informed decision with zero pressure.

FIVE TIPS TO MENTALLY PREPARE FOR SELLING YOUR HOME

As the old proverb goes, "Hope for the best and prepare for the worst." Here are five tips that I share with my clients. These are strategies that I have personally found helpful to me when I am mentally preparing for a challenge.

① **Be positive**

Yes, this can be tough to do if you are selling out of necessity, however it is imperative that you remain positive. Read inspirational books, attend church and prayer meetings and help others who are less fortunate than you. Be conscious of the negative thoughts that enter your mind and quickly dispel them. Maybe you can even give up watching the news during the selling process!

② **Get a coach**

Confide in a mentor or a close personal friend (with a level head). Spend a few minutes a week discussing your thoughts and feelings. In my real estate practice, I can help coach you throughout the process.

③ **Visualize the final outcome**

If you are moving by choice, spend some time seeing yourself and your family in your next home (after the dust has settled). If you are moving out of necessity, realize that there is light at the end of the tunnel and see yourself in that better light (living within your financial means, future opportunities, etc.).

④ Prayer and meditation

Studies have found that prayer and meditation are very beneficial when facing a stressful decision. Try spending 15 to 30 minutes in prayer and/or meditation each day.

⑤ Journal

Getting your thoughts out of your head and down on paper is a very freeing exercise. This will come as no challenge to you if you are constantly journaling. Others may find it easier to record their thoughts using a smart phone app or other device. Even if you simply voice your thoughts by speaking them aloud, it will help immensely. Ask yourself questions like, "What do I enjoy or not enjoy about this process?" or "What do I expect for the future in what I am doing now?"

If you're ready to begin your home selling journey, let's begin!

After selling numerous homes, I have observed that the three most important factors to selling your home are:

1. **Marketing**
2. **Price**
3. **Condition**

I will work with you to ensure that we have all of these key elements going for us in order to get your home SOLD in the least amount of time for the highest price. Let's take a close look at these elements in the following chapters.

"I am an old man and have known a great many troubles, but most of them never happened." — Mark Twain

NOTES:

CHALLENGE YOUR FEARS

In his book *The 4-Hour Work Week,* Timothy Ferris outlines what I consider to be a remarkable strategy for confronting your fear and stepping into action. This involves a question and answer (Q&A) session with yourself, where you **quickly write down your answers to the following questions,** spending just a few minutes on each answer. Don't think! Simply write down whatever comes to mind!

1. Define your nightmare, the absolute worst that could happen if you SOLD your home. What would be the permanent impact, if any, on a scale of 1–10?
2. What steps could you take to repair the damage or get things back on the upswing, even if temporarily?
3. What are the outcomes or benefits, both temporary and permanent, of more probable scenarios? Now that you've defined the nightmare, what are the more probable or definite positive outcomes?
4. What are you putting off out of fear? Usually, what we most fear doing is what we most need to do.
5. What is it costing you — financially, emotionally, and physically — to postpone action?

What are you waiting for? If you cannot answer this question without resorting to the previously rejected concept of *good timing,* the answer is simple: you are afraid, just like the rest of the world. Measure the cost of inaction, realize the unlikelihood and repairability of most missteps, and develop the most important habit of those who excel and enjoy doing so: action.

②

MARKETING YOUR HOME FOR SALE

The first key element to selling your home is marketing. I believe that marketing is about creating awareness in the minds of as many potential buyers as possible. Simply put, if buyers don't know about your home, it doesn't exist. Because I have spent a lot of time marketing homes, I understand what it takes to get your home SOLD. Every week I come across sellers who have tried listing their home with another agent only to find bitter disappointment. Let's examine why.

> **FACT**
>
> Every day homes expire from the market and fail to sell because they were not marketed correctly.

In the past seven years, computers and the internet have changed the face of real estate. Most agents haven't kept up. According to the National Association of REALTORS® (NAR) recent study, 90% of all home buyers now use the internet for house hunting. While most agents are struggling to keep up, my company has been immersed in the latest technology!

Besides not staying up to date with technology, less than 9% of agents are trained in the fine art of sales and marketing. That's because sales and marketing is nowhere in the training that agents receive in order to become licensed. The truth is most agents are good people; they just don't know how to do good marketing. Doing the kind of marketing that leads to a successful sale takes time, money and a great marketing plan.

The average agent in town uses a 3-point marketing plan. I call it the three P's of the average agent's marketing.

The average agent's marketing plan... (the 3 P's)

1. **P**ut a sign in the yard
2. **P**ut it on MLS
3. **P**ray that it will sell!

In my real estate practice, I employ the most comprehensive marketing plan you will find anywhere. I have a proven plan that will get your home SOLD faster and for more money by focusing my marketing efforts on five major categories 1) Outdoor Advertising, 2) Internet Advertising, 3) Print Advertising, 4) Premium Marketing and 5) Industry Marketing.

① **Outdoor Advertising**

- **Colorful Signage** — My signs are printed front and back, and they get noticed!
- **Direct Dial Number** — Buyers can call and get instant information from a live person.
- **24-hour Info Hotline** — Prospects can call 24 hours a

day and get information on your home. When a buyer calls, I receive a text notification that someone has called about your property. The text notification has their phone number so I can call them back right away and schedule a showing!

- **Full Color Virtual Flyers** — Your listing will be assigned its own QR code enabling buyers to pull the up-to-date home information right from their smart phone or mobile tablet. On my virtual flyers, I also include my buyer hotline where buyers can call and get info 24/7.

② **Internet Advertising**

I feature your home on hundreds of real estate search websites.

- **Brokerage Websites** — My technology allows us to showcase your property on every major brokerage website. This means that your home will be featured on sites like Keller Williams, RE/MAX, Coldwell Banker, and all the local "mom and pop" real estate outfits as well. So, even though you list with me, your home will be featured on just about every other brokerage site in town and throughout the nation.

- **National Channel Partners** — Through my unique relationship with my national channel partners, your home will be featured on popular websites like Zillow, Trulia, HGTV, Yahoo Homes, AOL Real Estate, Oodle and many more.
- **Affiliate Channel Partners** — Popular websites like those sponsored by Fannie Mae, Freddie Mac and many others will also feature your home.
- **Regional Channel Partners** — I market on hundreds of popular regional websites.
- **Craigslist** — I list and update your property on Craigslist regularly. My well-constructed ads generate a steady stream of buyer inquiries every day.
- **Search Engine Optimization (SEO)** — Of course you are familiar with search engines like Google, Yahoo and MSN, etc. Your listing will be keyword optimized by my industry professional so that your home achieves high ranking status on the internet's most popular search engines.
- **Social Media** — I use Facebook, YouTube and many other popular social media platforms to market your property. I have lots of friends on my Facebook profile where your

listing will be prominently featured along with my YouTube channel and several other key social platforms.

③ **Print Advertising**

- **Just Listed Cards** — I mail color postcards to your closest neighbors letting your community help spread the word.
- **Real Estate Magazines** — I prominently feature your home in real estate magazines carried at local restaurants and grocery stores.
- **Monthly Mailings** — I periodically direct mail to local residents and my database marketing my website that prominently displays your home as a premier featured listing.

④ **Premium Marketing**

- **'Featured Listing' Exposure** — Your home is featured prominently on my website in my Featured Properties section.
- **Professional Photographs** — When buyers are browsing the internet to search for properties, photographs do more to help sell your property than anything else. That's why I hire a professional photographer to take high-quality photos of your property.

- **Virtual Tour** — On my larger listings, I pay for a professional 360° panoramic virtual tour featuring several key areas of your home.

- **My Monthly e-Newsletter** — Each month my e-newsletter is sent to my database of clients and my sphere of influence promoting the site where your home is prominently featured .
- **Electronic Feedback System** — Whenever your home is shown, I send an electronic survey to the showing agent. I encourage the agents to provide feedback on the showing so that you know exactly what buyers are thinking and saying about your home.

⑤ Industry Marketing

When you list your home with me you get a lot more than just me!

- My company's agents are working for you. It's true. That means I can tap into all of the agents at my brokerage who are ready, willing and able to show and sell your home the minute any of their buyer prospects show an interest.
- Our entire MLS member agents are working for you. I mobilize all of these agents with my targeted marketing campaigns designed to provide them the exact information they need to get their potential buyers excited about seeing your home.

I don't miss a beat when it comes to marketing your home; I spare NO expense. If there is anything else that you think I should add to the marketing of your home, just let me know!

③

PRICING YOUR HOME

Now, let's spend some time examining the second key element to selling your home — price.

After spending many hours studying the local area market, comparing it with the national market and reviewing recent sales data, I have come to understand that pricing a home is more of an art form than a science.

When it comes to pricing your home, there are a lot of opinions, but only one set of facts. Together, we will examine the facts of record to determine the most effective pricing strategy to obtain the maximum price possible for you. Price can sometimes be a moving target. That's why it is so important for me to understand what the market is doing and how the market is currently trending (shifting up, down, or staying flat).

HOW PRICE IS DETERMINED

Price is determined by what a buyer is willing to pay for a home. Ultimately, at the end of the day, market price is set by the buyer. Therefore, it is imperative for me to research to discover exactly what buyers are currently paying for a home as similar to yours as possible.

Let's say a buyer is willing to pay $415,000 for a home in a certain area. The buyer and seller agree on the price, the transaction moves forward and ultimately the home closes. Once the sales price is published, the SOLD price is then used as a comparable factor for all future home sales of similar homes in the area. Let's suppose the market takes a downturn and buyers are no longer willing to pay $415,000 but $390,000 for the same home. As the market begins to shift downward, the sold data will begin reflecting lower sold prices which will then reset the current market value. The same happens when the market shifts upward. Higher sales prices replace the lower home sales data.

In my practice, I use a large pool of information to determine what buyers are currently willing to pay for a home similar to yours. Also, by showing you the market trends in your neighborhood, I enable you to determine whether it makes more sense to sell now or to wait.

GETTING A CMA (COMPARATIVE MARKET ANALYSIS)

A CMA is an extremely helpful tool that I use to determine what the market is saying. The CMA is a side-by-side comparison report of homes currently for sale and homes that have SOLD in the same neighborhood or area as yours. I will typically include new listings (for sale), pending sales (under contract), closed sales (solds) and expired listings (failed to sell).

CMAs can vary widely depending on the knowledge, skill level and experience of the agent inputting the search parameters, as well as the data fields that are chosen. This is a delicate and critical job that will help you achieve maximum success. You do not want to trust getting this information from the wrong agent, and you certainly don't want to trust an online source that spits out un-scrubbed and unverified data.

Because I work and live in the area, I have had the opportunity to become intimately familiar with our local area neighborhoods.

So what does that mean for you? It means that every week I am gaining more experience that I can put to work for you! This puts me in the best position to help educate you on what the market is doing, how the market is trending, and how to get the most for your home in the least amount of time. Achieving these results does not happen by chance. I am very purposeful about achieving the successful sale of every home I list. I also want to net my clients more than they would get by listing with anyone else.

In order to get the most accurate pricing data on your home and net you the most money, I have purchased and use the most sophisticated software systems in the industry.

After starting with the right tools, I examine the data using my experience. Then, I take the following factors into consideration:

Location

When building your CMA, I will endeavor to use comparables from your neighborhood. Besides that, I will also pull a report of every home that SOLD on your street in the past year so that I can review some specific trending data.

Size

Generally speaking, I try to keep the comparable properties to within 10% of the size of your home.

Age

When collecting the data, I try to select comparables that are the exact same age as your home or within just a few years.

Other Details

There are quite a few other parameters that I search through in order to get the most accurate results, including number of bedrooms, bathrooms, garage spaces, living areas, number of stories and more.

Review of Each Comparable

After I compile and aggregate the data, I painstakingly go through each comparable property and review the photographs and property descriptions. This helps me assess the condition of each property to see if they are aesthetically and physically comparable with your home. This exercise helps me better select the best comparables. I will sometimes drive through your neighborhood and make a visual analysis of the comparables.

Trending

After carefully analyzing all of the data, I then take a look at how your neighborhood prices are trending (both monthly, quarterly and over the past 6–12 months). This final analysis helps us learn whether market prices are going up, holding steady or creeping downward.

Analyzing the Data

Once I have completed your CMA, the next step is for us to analyze and review the data together.

> **FACT**
>
> When it comes to pricing, market trends are constantly changing. Working with the wrong agent will cost you time, aggravation and you could be leaving money on the table.

As I mentioned in chapter one, the three things that sell homes are 1) Marketing, 2) Price, and 3) Condition. As you saw in the previous chapter, I employ the most comprehensive marketing plan you will find. I am not shy about spending all the money it takes to get you maximum exposure and the maximum sale price possible. Once I have comprehensively analyzed all the data, and made a visual inspection of your property, I can look at the critical step of setting your price.

Pricing Strategy Meeting

Although most sellers expect me to tell them what I think the price of their home should be, they are pleasantly surprised by my pricing system. You see, I believe that my role is to provide the best education to my clients on what the market is doing in their area. I do this by conducting a 30-minute Pricing Strategy Meeting with my sellers before we sign the listing paperwork. This is a free, no obligation consultation.

This meeting is a fun, but very serious and informative session. We will first review the marketing plan for getting your home SOLD. We then spend several minutes reviewing the comprehensive CMA. Armed with the right information, I then let my clients set the price that they feel comfortable with. My job is then to get you the price you want (within reason). After we set the price, if you are comfortable and confident that I can sell your home, the paperwork takes about 10 minutes.

OTHER FACTORS

Absorption Rate

By studying the number of active listings compared to the number of SOLDs in your neighborhood, I am able to determine what I call the absorption rate of your property. This information will help us project how many months of like inventory there is on the market, how quickly your home will sell, and where the market is headed.

Affordability Index

This measurement tool was developed by the National Association of REALTORS® and has become one of the most important mechanisms for describing and tracking the condition of residential real estate markets. The index relates home prices in the market to consumer level economic factors that are indicators, or determinants, of purchasing power.

It does this by dividing median family income in our local market by qualifying income required to purchase the median priced home. Knowing the affordability index in our area allows me to understand the potential buyer pool for your home.

How the Buyer's Appraisal Will Affect Price

It is important to understand that most buyers will be using some form of financing when they purchase your home. This means that the buyer's lender will order an appraisal on your property. If the home does not appraise for at least the amount of the sale price, the buyer's loan will be rejected. This is often true even if the buyer is putting a large amount of cash down on the property. This is one of the major reasons why you will need to set the right price on your home.

If the buyer's appraiser is wrong however, you can rest assured that I will challenge the appraisal. I am often able to articulate and prove value by sharing data, amenities and upgrades that can easily be overlooked.

Buyer's Market vs. Seller's Market

Simply put, a Buyer's Market is when supply (number of homes for sale) outpaces demand, and a Seller's Market is when demand outpaces supply. Put another way, in a buyer's market there are more homes than there are buyers, and in a seller's market there are fewer homes than there are buyers.

How Pricing Affects Showings

Research has proven that price drives traffic through a listing, and that pricing a property correctly at the beginning of the listing process will attract the most potential buyers to your home. Fewer visits result in fewer opportunities to receive a contract.

PRICING MY UNIQUE AND LUXURY PROPERTIES

For homes that are very rare and unique, I will often recommend that we also order an appraisal by a licensed appraiser. While I use the same criteria, software and systems as most appraisers, the appraiser will be seen by the buyer and the buyer's lender as a very credible source, when it is very difficult to clearly see the value of your property. I employ this strategy on my properties that are on 1+ acres, my luxury inventory line (homes priced at $1 Million+) and other unique homes.

OTHER PRICING STRATEGIES

As-Is Pricing

The "As Is" pricing strategy is for sellers who lack the funds, ability or desire to properly prepare their home for sale.

After having your home inspected by a licensed home inspector, you can review the report and get any bids on the work needed. You can then properly price your home based on accurate knowledge of its condition.

"Hot Property" Pricing Strategy

This pricing strategy is particularly effective in all types of markets.

Generally, with this strategy, you get a pre-sale property inspection report, correct all the items that are affordable, and then put

FACT

The **BEST** chance for selling your property is within the **FIRST 7 WEEKS.** Studies show that the longer a property stays on the market, the less the seller will net. Let's price it right.

the property on the market at or near the lowest price you're willing to accept for the property. In the right market, multiple offers may be possible using this strategy.

THE BEST CHANCE FOR SELLING YOUR PROPERTY IS WITHIN THE FIRST SEVEN WEEKS. STUDIES SHOW THAT THE LONGER A PROPERTY STAYS ON THE MARKET, THE LESS THE SELLER WILL NET.

The right price is important.

* A property generates the most interest when it first hits the market.
* The number of showings is greatest during this time if it is priced at a realistic market value.
* Starting at a higher list price and dropping the price later misses the excitement and fails to generate strong activity.
* Many homes that start high end up expiring, canceling or selling below market value.

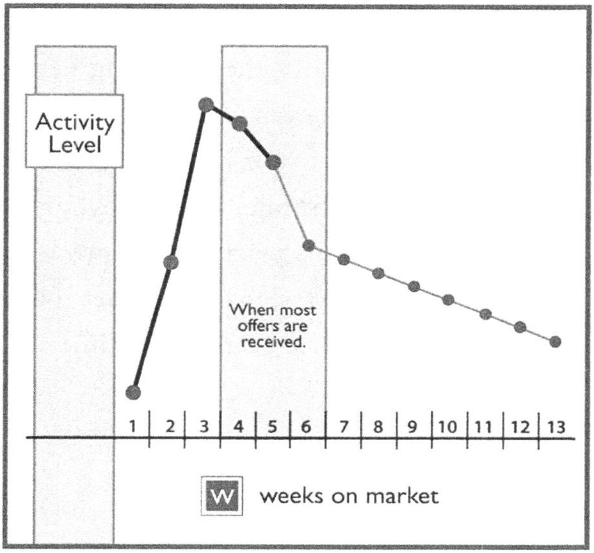

Pricing Strategy Pyramid

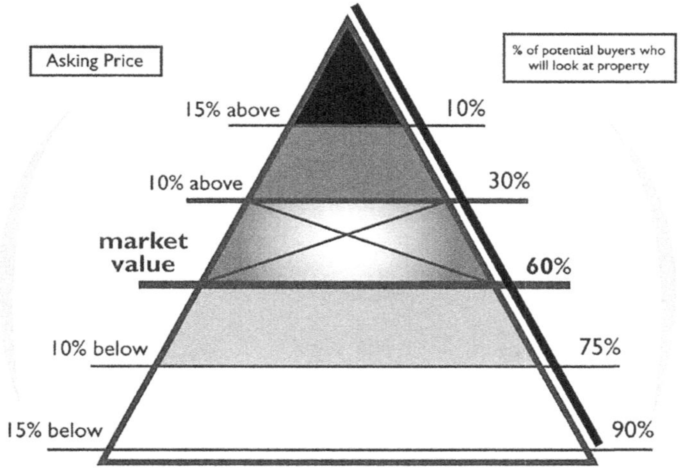

It is very important to price your property at a competitive market value at the signing of the listing agreement. The market is so competitive that even overpricing by a few thousand dollars could mean that your house will have difficulty selling. Interestingly, your first offer is usually your best offer. Below are several reasons for pricing your property at the market value right from the start in order to net you the most amount of money in the shortest amount of time

An Overpriced Home...

1. Minimizes offers
2. Lowers agent response
3. Limits qualified buyers
4. Lowers showings
5. Lowers prospects
6. Limits financing
7. Wastes advertising dollars
8. Nets less for the seller

④

GETTING YOUR HOME READY FOR THE MARKET

Now we've come to the third key element in selling your home; getting it in "show condition."

Getting your property ready for the market begins with a truthful and honest assessment of your property's current condition. The way your home looked while you lived in and enjoyed it may be very different from how your home will look during the selling process. If my clients will be occupying the home during the selling process, I advise them to strike that delicate balance between homeowner comfort and stellar showcasing.

In my practice, homes that are 1) marketed correctly, 2) priced properly, and 3) prepped for sale (and well-staged) sell faster than all the others. Proper preparation allows us to sell your home in the least amount of time and for the most money. This winning strategy also results in the least amount of inconvenience to you because your home will only be 'on the market' for a short time (often less than 30 days) before it goes under contract. Don't worry! I never advocate spending a lot of money during this process. Unless your home is in grave disrepair, the time and money spent to get your home ready for market will be nominal.

In my opinion, the single most important thing you can do in the preparation process is to de-clutter your home. Once your home is de-cluttered, the next items are cleaning and painting. These three items will not cost very much or take much time, but you will be surprised by the difference doing them will make.

MY BIG 3 TIPS TO PREP YOUR HOME

De-clutter • Clean • Paint

1. **De-clutter.** When you think about the idea of de-cluttering, think of floor space and counter space. Generally, you will want to display the maximum amount of floor space and the maximum amount of countertop space. As you look around at the floors and counter spaces (including tabletops, desks, etc.) of your home, identify things that don't belong. Then make these areas as clear as possible. If you have large pieces of furniture that are taking up a big chunk of floor space and can be eliminated, consider putting those items in storage or storing them in your garage. The more uncluttered and unencumbered floor space the buyer can see, the larger and more inviting your home will feel.

2. **Clean.** A good deep clean is an absolute necessity after you have removed the clutter. This involves cleaning your home both inside and out. The floors, walls, baseboards, doors and all surfaces in your home should be thoroughly cleaned. If possible, the outside of your home and the driveways and walkways should be power washed. When it comes to cleaning, I recommend that you either form a cleaning crew (you and 3 or more friends) or better yet, simply hire a cleaning service. A good deep clean should cost around $150–$200 or so, depending on the size and condition of your home. For the power washing, I recommend you hire a reputable contractor.
3. **Paint.** Once your home is de-cluttered and clean, it's time to slap on some paint! Take a good look at all of the walls, baseboards, doors, window sills and ceilings around your home. In some cases they will just need to be touched up here and there; other areas will need to be entirely repainted. Be objective and make a list. Then decide whether or not you will do the work yourself or hire someone. At $20 or less per gallon, paint is probably the least expensive way to make a dramatic improvement to your home.

HOME REPAIRS

I strongly encourage sellers to complete any minor and cosmetic home repairs that you can afford to. These include

things like broken light fixtures, replacing light bulbs, torn screens, cracked caulking, broken tiles, leaking faucets, cracked windows, loose doorknobs, etc.

While you and your family may have been perfectly content to live with these minor items, they are a red flag to prospective homebuyers. Home buyers generally suspect that homes with small items in disrepair will likely have bigger items that have not been addressed. It's fairly easy to compile a list of things that need to be done and then pay a handyman to complete this list of minor repairs in less than a day. I have a comprehensive list of reputable trades I can recommend to you. What if you can't afford to do repairs? No worries. We will simply use my "As-Is" pricing strategy from Chapter 3.

DIGGING DEEPER (GETTING A PRE-INSPECTION)

For sellers who want to go one step further, a pre-sale home inspection can be ordered.

In my real estate practice, I have observed that more homes fall "out of contract" due to the results of the home inspection than for any other reason. For homes that are older than 10 years, getting a pre-sale home inspection is a good idea. The cost will generally be around $300 to $400. The inspection report will uncover any minor or major issues with your home

I have observed that the #1 reason homes fall out of contract is due to issues arising from the inspection report. Having your home pre-inspected helps you avoid this disappointment.

and should be considered a small investment paying to protect yourself from the potential of a large future disappointment. Even if you do not plan to fix the items uncovered in a home inspection report, just knowing and disclosing what the issues are will better prepare you for the negotiating process.

STAGING

While de-cluttering, cleaning, painting and minor repairs will *prepare* your home for sale, staging is the process of *showcas-*

ing your home for sale. According to a 2011 study conducted by the Real Estate Staging Association (RESA), homes that previously failed to sell SOLD in 73% less time after they were professionally staged. The study was conducted with 174 vacant and occupied homes. Those homes averaged 156 days on the market without a contract before the homeowners decided to have them professionally staged. After staging, those same homes SOLD in an average of 42 days.

Another study by RESA of 410 professionally staged homes concluded that these homes SOLD 79% faster than similar homes that were not staged.

7 Seller Benefits to Staging Your Home

1. Professionally staged homes present and show better than competing houses for sale, including new construction homes and higher-priced houses.
2. Staged properties will sell faster when compared with houses that have not been staged. From the date of listing until the day of closing, home staging shortens this time frame, even in a slow real estate market.
3. Staged properties can increase the number of offers and selling price in hot markets.
4. Buyers view professionally staged listings as "well-maintained."
5. Buyers' agents recognize that professionally staged listings are "move-in" ready and are inclined to show staged properties.

6. Photos of professionally staged listings look better on the MLS, as well as in print.
7. Professionally staged listings "STAND-OUT" in prospective buyers' minds.

(Source: Real Estate Staging Association)

NOTES:

____

____

____

MORE TIPS ON SELLING YOUR HOME

The First Impression Counts...Make It a Positive One!

The most important single reason that a home sells is its emotional appeal. Over 90% of buyers in today's market buy on emotion. Looking at your house through "buyer's eyes" can help you prepare your home to sell for the best price in the least amount of time. When you begin preparing your home, begin outside and work your way in. Make up a "to do" list as you go along keeping in mind the importance of first impressions.

Exterior Tips

It's estimated that more than half of all houses are SOLD before buyers even get out of their cars. Stand across the street from your home and review its "curb appeal." What can you do to improve the very first impression?

- Keep sidewalks and patios hosed off. Hose down house siding to remove cobwebs and dirt. Hose down your garage and clean your driveway of any grease spots. A garage can be an important selling point for your home, and a good spraying with a garden hose and just a drop of industrial strength cleaner can make a big difference.
- Mow, trim, weed, and water lawns and gardens. Add a fresh layer of mulch or gravel if needed and plant flowers for color.
- The front door is one of the first things prospective buyers see. If it shows signs of wear, clean, stain, or paint it.
- Make sure the doorbell and porch lights work.
- Remove trash and debris from the yard and around house.
- Remove extra vehicles from view.
- Repair any fences or gates.
- Remove holiday lights that may still be hanging.
- Paint exterior window sashes, trim, and shutters (repainting the entire exterior can be an expensive and unnecessary venture, unless there is bad blistering or peeling.)
- Apply fresh paint to wooden fences.

- Buy a new welcome mat.
- Place potted flowers near the door.
- Clean windows inside and out.
- Power wash the home's exterior.
- Ensure gutters and downspouts are firmly attached and functioning.

Interior Tips

When showing your home to prospective buyers, you want to make everything look spacious, organized, bright, warm, and "homey." Start with a full housecleaning from top to bottom. Don't let dirt and clutter obscure your home's good points. A clean home will sell a lot faster than a dirty one.

- Be sure walls are clean and free of dirt and fingerprints. Consider a fresh coat of paint if washing doesn't do the trick.
- Wash all windows and sills.
- Curtains and drapes should be freshly cleaned.
- Arrange furniture to make rooms appear spacious and attractive.
- Evaluate the furniture in each room and remove anything that interrupts the flow or makes the room appear smaller. Consider renting a storage unit to move the items off-site.
- Clean all light fixtures and ceiling fans.
- Have carpets cleaned.
- Make minor repairs.

- Replace any burned out light bulbs. You can make rooms seem warmer and brighter by using high intensity light bulbs that give the house a warm glow.
- Discard or replace any dying houseplants.

Kitchen & Bath Tips

The bathrooms and kitchen are focal points for most buyers. Be sure those rooms are clean and uncluttered.

- Clear extra appliances, accessories, etc. from counters.
- Polish sinks and remove stains.
- Clean appliances thoroughly inside and out.
- Straighten and remove excess papers from the kitchen memo area.
- Clean out your cabinets and drawers. Add shelf paper and utensil trays to make them look as organized as possible.
- Buy a new shower curtain.

Decluttering Tips

Eliminating clutter will give your home a more spacious look. By removing or storing things you don't need, you create a roomy, comfortable feeling that will be inviting to prospective buyers. If a house is too cluttered, buyers have trouble imagining themselves and their belongings in it. Remember, when in doubt, move it out!

- Clean out closets to display their roominess. Prospective buyers love to inspect for storage space; so, it's important to make closets look as spacious as possible. Another trick is to clear the floor space in closets. This simple strategy will make the closet appear as large as possible.

- Be sure clothes are hung neatly and shoes and other objects are neatly arranged. If something you have stored away hasn't been worn or used in the last year, chances are it never will be. Give it away, sell it, or pack it neatly in a box and store it in the garage.
- Have a garage sale! Not only will you be reducing clutter, you can use the money to finance your touch-ups.
- Straighten bookshelves and remove unnecessary papers from coffee tables.
- In children's rooms, straighten or store extra toys and remove distracting posters. Arrange toys to look fun and inviting. Open a book on a night stand. Add a flowering plant and arrange decorative pillows or shams on the bed.
- If you have a spare room or storage area, turn it into an area with a purpose. If it's too small to be a bedroom, turn it into a hobby center, study or office.
- Again, consider renting storage space to move out items you won't need before you move.

Cleaning Tips

When a home is clean, it gives the impression that it has been well cared for. Some fresh paint and a one-time professional cleaning service can make your house look like new.

- Be sure every room smells as good as it looks, paying special attention to pet areas, children's nurseries and bathrooms.
- Polish all brass and chrome fixtures.
- Polish mirrors so they sparkle.
- Scrub and wax floors.
- Have carpets professionally cleaned and deodorized.
- Clean and deodorize garbage areas.
- Clean sliding door track so that the door moves quietly and smoothly.

Repairing Tips

Making little repairs can make a big difference. Although many families learn to live with a broken doorknob or a cracked window, all of these little things should be fixed when selling your home. The savvy homeowner concentrates his efforts on cosmetic repairs that cost relatively little, but return a lot on the investment (don't forget those first impressions!).

- Repair leaking faucets, running toilets, grout, and caulking as needed.
- Replace any cracked windows and torn screens.
- Patch and paint wall and ceiling cracks.
- Repair or replace loose doorknobs, drawer pulls, sticking doors and windows, warped drawers, cabinet handles, towel racks, switch plates and outlet covers.

- Tack down any loose molding and glue down any lifted wallpaper.

Neutralizing

Try to create an appearance that allows the buyers to picture themselves living there. Neutral paint, décor and carpeting create a home for any life style.

- Eliminate distracting colors and accessories so that buyers can concentrate on positive impressions.
- Brighten things with fresh paint. White, off-white, or beige walls make a room look bigger and lighter. Interior painting costs very little and it can make a big difference in a buyer's perception. Go ahead and do it.

Don't Over Improve

Preparing your home for sale doesn't need to be expensive or time-consuming as long as you keep up with normal maintenance. In the event you do not have the time to do the cleaning or repair work, consider hiring a professional; it could save you time and money later. A few hundred dollars well spent can be the best investment you'll ever make. Remember, you need to think like a buyer now and have a critical eye.

Use caution in planning any major improvements that you think will enable you to get more for the house than you paid for it. Most people shopping for a house would rather plan their own major changes. You are usually wiser to sell them the potential at a price they can afford.

5

CHOOSING THE RIGHT AGENT

Once you have made the decision to sell, finding the right agent is next on the agenda. As many sellers have experienced the hard way, not all real estate agents are created equal!

Think about it this way: If you had to undergo an important surgery, you would certainly search for the right surgeon. More than likely, you would look for a specialist with many years of experience, one that had performed hundreds or even thousands of successful procedures. In the same way, selling your home is a serious matter. You don't want to trust anyone but the right agent with your biggest asset.

PICK THE BEST

Suppose you had to have a risky heart operation. Let's further suppose that this was a life or death operation and the chances of success were 50/50, depending mostly on which doctor you chose. Keep in mind that all of the doctors you researched charge similar rates. If you could choose any doctor you wanted, wouldn't you choose the best?

Unfortunately, some homeowners don't use the same amount of discretion when selecting an agent. When you pick the wrong agent, you net less money, have a less than stellar experience. Also, it will take longer to sell than necessary.

Let's take a real life example that I have seen played out many times. Mr. and Mrs. Williams needed to sell their home. They made the mistake of hiring the first agent that came along. They had a terrible experience and their home never sold. They then decided to sell it themselves! After picking the wrong agent, they were a bit skittish and figured they could do a much better job. Big mistake. Although they had a lot of tire kickers, there were no serious offers. After several months of frustration, they then did the research and decided to hire a listing specialist. After hiring the right agent, they were able to achieve a successful sale and get more than 98% of our asking price. That was when they learned the value of hiring the right agent.

DO YOU PLAN ON INTERVIEWING MORE THAN ONE AGENT FOR THE JOB OF SELLING YOUR HOME?

If so, be sure to ask the right questions. In fact, whenever a prospective seller tells me they are interviewing several agents, I always ask these sellers two key questions: 1) How did you go about choosing the agents that you plan to interview? 2) What interview questions are you asking these agents?

> **FACT**
>
> There is a HUGE difference between an agent who specializes in buyers and one who specializes in listings. As a listing specialist, I can get your home sold faster and for top dollar.

When it comes to choosing the right agent, just imagine you have the opportunity to win $1 million. All you have to do is shoot (and land) one free-throw basketball shot. The downside: you only get one shot! However, according to the rules, you can pick anyone you want to make that shot for you. Who would you choose? How would you go about choosing the person to make that million dollar shot?

More than likely, you would decide that you were going to choose a professional NBA player. Then you would research each player's statistics as to their free throw average. You would then pick the person with the best average, giving you the best chance for success.

The process of choosing the right agent is exactly the same. By choosing me to sell your home, you can greatly increase your chances of success.

SELECT A LISTING SPECIALIST VS. A BUYER SPECIALIST

In the real estate game, the overwhelming majority of agents specialize in working with buyers. I am a Listing Specialist, and I specialize in working with Sellers. This unique specialization has enabled us to focus on and employ the best techniques for getting your home SOLD. When choosing the right agent to sell your home, you want to select a Listing Specialist.

SELLING YOUR HOME YOURSELF

For a variety of reasons, some sellers choose to try to sell their home themselves. Using my previous analogy, this would be the equivalent of trying to make the $1 million shot by yourself. For most, this proves to be a losing proposition. The statistical facts prove that homeowners will net a lot less money, and take a lot longer to sell when trying to sell their home themselves, instead of hiring me to get it SOLD.

According to NAR's For Sale By Owner (FSBO) 2012 Statistics, 9% of U.S. homes sold FSBO. Knowing what goes into a top dollar sale, it's not surprising that the data reveals the typical FSBO home sold for 18.65% less than similar properties that were properly marketed and exposed by a licensed REALTOR®.

Let's examine why this is the case. When a person decides to represent themselves in a court of law, the opposing attorney will have an advantage. In the same way, prospective buyers will have an advantage over someone trying to sell their own home.

The #1 reason some sellers try to sell on their own is to get out of paying the agent commission. Because I statistically net 8–9% more for my clients, they would actually lose money, and time, trying to sell themselves. Let's take a quick look: Suppose you decided to sell your home and the agent commission was 6%. Most FSBOs believe they are saving that 6% by selling themselves, but let's look at the facts.

> **FACT**
>
> **FSBO Fact**
>
> Last year, the average for sale by owner (FSBO) home SOLD for 18.65% less than one properly marketed by a top REALTOR®.

In most cases, the FSBO will agree to pay a 3% (or so) commission to the buyer agent who finds a buyer for the home. This means the 'perceived' savings is now 3%. However, when you take into account the fact that homes properly marketed generate an 8 to 19% higher sales price, it becomes apparent that selling yourself can actually net you 5 to 16% less than hiring us to do everything for you!

THE PERILS OF HIRING A DISCOUNT BROKER

There are several companies in town that offer to sell your home for a discounted fee. Most sellers don't need to be advised about the many potential perils they will face by putting their home on the market with a bargain-basement operation. Still, let's take a closer look at this strategy.

For some time, there was a discount brokerage I heard about that would advertise a 1% commission. From the onset, the advertisement was misleading. In fact, the one percent was for the listing agent and did not include a 3% commission that you were expected to pay to the buyer's agent. In reality the total commission was 4%. What many sellers did not realize was that the agents with this company only had an average sale price of 91.3% to 94.7% of list price. When you do the math, it is clear that by hiring me, you can net up to 7% more than you could with a discount broker! Most sellers will actually lose money by hiring a "discount" agent, and they will increase their time on the market and their aggravation.

My experience shows that discount agents provide the least amount of support in the areas you need them the most. Ask yourself this question: Why would a heart doctor discount his services? Generally speaking, it would be because he is either inexperienced (and needs patients to practice on), or not 'good enough' to compete with doctors who charge regular or premium rates. That's the guy you don't want operating on you.

It's unfortunate that discount agents are seen as the *garage sale* of the real estate industry. When agents are out showing prospective buyers homes and they see a discount agent's sign in the yard, they will instinctively want to offer a 'discount price' for that home.

Let's examine why this is the case. Suppose you had an expensive watch. If you place that watch in the fine jewelry showcase of a department store, it will be priced at top dollar, and buyers will gladly pay the price it's offered for because of the product presentation, the skills of the knowledgeable salesperson, and the perceived quality. Now, let's take that same watch and put it at a garage sale. Do you think it will sell for the same price it could command from the fine jewelry showcase? At a garage sale, not only will buyers expect to pay far less for the same watch in the same condition, they will instinctively believe that the watch is worth less than the value marked on it. That's because the watch is at a garage sale. The same effect happens when your home is marketed through a discount agency.

HOW COMMISSIONS WORK

Many sellers understand that I charge a commission, but are a little unclear about how that commission is divided after I earn it.

Let's say we sell your home and my fee is 6%. The first thing I would do with my earnings is pay the buyer's agent (the agent who brings a buyer) half of it. That leaves me with 3%. 1% of that goes to my brokerage. I have chosen to align myself with the top real estate company in the area, which further helps to provide maximum exposure for your property. Another 1% goes toward marketing your home and servicing your listing. That leaves me with 1% for myself, which is what I live on. And from my 1%, I have to pay taxes!

NOTES:

How Realtors are paid...

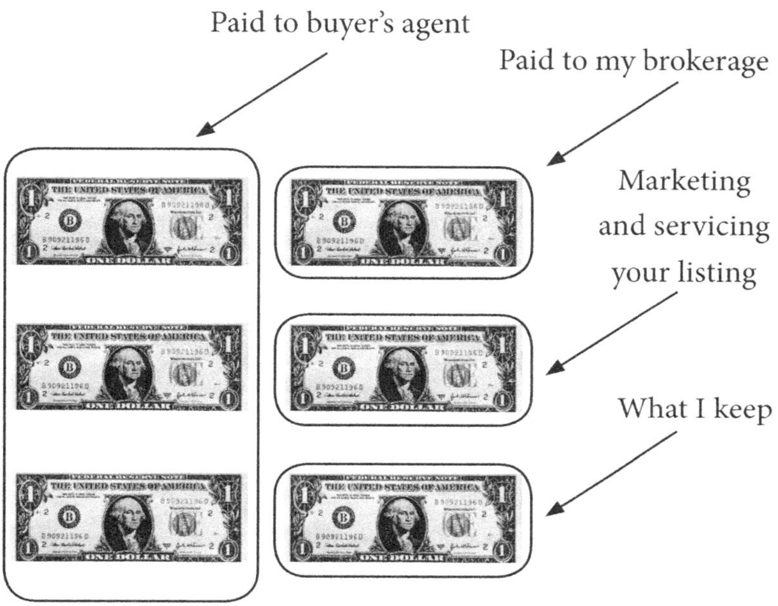

⑥

HANDLING SHOWINGS

Now that we have your home on the market, let's move forward and get it SOLD!

It is important to make your home as easy to show as possible. If your home is vacant, this will obviously be easy since buyers can look at it without notice and you don't have to prep for every showing. If your home is occupied, providing buyers with a hassle-free showing process is a bit more challenging.

Keep in mind that when buyers are out looking at properties, they may be viewing several homes that particular day. That's because most buyers view homes in "batches" (3 today in your area and 4 tomorrow in another area). If they are asking to view your home at a particular time, it usually means that they will be in your area within that time frame. If you do not allow your home to be one of the properties viewed, it may be eliminated from their list.

This is why I always recommend that, although it may be inconvenient, you should allow your home to be viewed (and be prepped for viewings) whenever possible, within reason.

If you have circumstances that do not allow you to leave your home quickly (you work from home, take care of an elderly parent or small children, etc.), we can place special instructions on MLS like "seller requests 2-hour notice prior to showing." Unless your home is unique and/or particularly desirable, I do not suggest you set your showings up by appointment only.

SHOWING WITH RENTERS

I have found that homes currently rented create a new set of challenges when it comes to showing. Tenants are often uncomfortable with the idea of allowing the home to be shown and can make the showing process more arduous. If buyers are having a difficult time getting in to see the property, you will have a difficult time getting it sold.

My advice is to enlist the cooperation of your tenants. Try to offer them some kind of incentive for cooperating during the showing process. Perhaps you can give them $20 off their rent for every showing, or something creative like that.

Another challenge to showing a tenant occupied property is that the tenants will likely not have the home in "show" condition because they are not personally vested in the successful sale of the property. In some cases they could even be working against you, if selling the home has a negative impact on their moving time frame. Again, my advice is to seek the cooperation of your tenant. Give them my list of tips for showing the house and offer them an incentive for their cooperation.

MY TOP TIPS ON SHOWING THE HOUSE

When it's time for a buyer's agent to show your home, all your preparations will be worth the effort. Here are a few final tips that can add that extra touch.

- The television and radio should be turned off. Let the buyer's agent and buyer talk free of disturbances.
- Send children and pets outdoors to play. This will eliminate confusion and keep the prospect's attention focused on your home.
- Be absent during showings. Many prospects feel like intruders when owners/occupants are present. They tend to hurry away or fail to ask their agent the questions they'd really like to ask. Your absence will put buyers at ease and give them a chance to spend more time looking at your home and absorbing its advantages.
- Leave drapes open for light and airiness. If it's evening, all lights should be turned on to give the rooms a larger appearance and a cheerful effect.
- Be sure the kitchen sink is free of dishes and rooms are uncluttered. Make sure trash baskets are empty.
- Make sure rugs are clean and straight. Set a comfortable temperature. Do a "once-over" cleaning—vacuum, sweep, and dust. Finally, check every room.

- If you are at home during the showing, be courteous, but don't force conversation with the potential buyer. They want to inspect your house, not pay a social call.
- Open windows to freshen rooms. Set tables with flowers and linens.
- Never apologize for the appearance of your home. After all, it has been lived in.
- The buyer's agent knows the buyer's requirements and can better emphasize the features of your home when you don't follow along. You will be called, if needed.
- Let me discuss price, terms, possession and other factors with the customer. I am better qualified to bring negotiations to a favorable conclusion.
- If buyers just drop by and aren't accompanied by a real estate agent, it's best not to show your home. Ask for their names and phone number, and provide it to us for follow-up. (Most agents screen clients so you don't waste time showing to someone who isn't qualified or worse, a potential burglar.)
- I use an electronic keybox system that agents must access in order to obtain the key. This keybox records which agent showed your home (and the exact time and date), so that I can track all showings and request feedback.

⑦

WORKING WITH OFFERS

Once I list your home for sale, I will soon be calling you and saying "We have an offer!"

So let's discuss how I work with offers to achieve a win-win for both you and the buyer. Sometimes my sellers can have the mistaken notion that the buyer is the adversary in the negotiating process. After all, the buyer wants to get your home for the lowest price possible and you want to get the highest price, right?

While that may be true, I take a different approach. I believe that the buyer and my seller are allies in the transaction since they both have the same objective. My seller wants to sell the home and the buyer wants to acquire it. This means that a successful sale achieves the goals of both the buyer and seller.

Once we receive an offer on your home, I will run a revised CMA so you can see exactly what the market in your neighborhood is doing at the time the offer is received. Then, you and I will review the offer together and I'll point out the various factors to take into consideration. I will also run a *Seller's Estimated Net Sheet* showing you what your net proceeds will be based on the offer submitted. After you have looked at all the information and weighed my counsel, you will be in a position to either accept the offer or counter the offer.

REVIEWING THE OFFER

The first thing I will want you to do is review the offer. Here are the main points of the offer/contract that I will review with you:

Sales Price

The offer shows the amount that the buyer is offering for your home, and is, no doubt, the most important information to us. The offer also shows how much cash the buyer will be putting down; an important factor when considering multiple offers.

Financing

Knowing how the buyer intends to structure his financing and what type of loan he is approved for is very helpful. Of course I always verify that the buyer is pre-approved to purchase your property. If there is any question or doubt, even after we receive the pre-approval letter, I will ask my preferred lender to contact the buyer's lender and ask critical questions that will validate whether or not the buyer is creditworthy.

Even though the buyer has been pre-approved for the loan, the actual loan process takes several weeks. If the buyer's lender uncovers a previously undiscovered credit issue during that time frame the deal could be in jeopardy. That's why my bulletproof process ensures that we are working with a solid buyer from the onset.

Escrow

Here, the buyer is agreeing to deposit what some call 'earnest money.' This amount is held in escrow by the title company, escrow company or attorney that will close the transaction. The earnest money also gives you some security if the buyer defaults on the deal. There may be some exceptions to this rule, which I can discuss with you in greater detail.

Closing

This contract also contains the proposed closing date. Most closing dates are set for 30 to 45 days in the future. When reviewing the offer, we will discuss whether or not the proposed closing date works for you.

Closing Costs

On every transaction, the seller has their own closing costs (sales commission, title policy, escrow costs and recording fees, etc.). The buyer has closing costs as well (loan origination, prepaid expenses, etc.). It is not uncommon for the buyer to "roll in" some or all of his closing costs when putting an offer together.

Rather than focusing on the amount the buyer is asking you to pay on his behalf, it is better to focus on your "net offer." Your net offer is the sales price offered (para 3) less buyer expenses (para 12). For example, let's say you are asking $450,000 for your home and you receive an offer of $445,000 and para 12 contains an amount of $5,000. Your net offer is $440,000. Remember, I'll help you navigate through all of this and help you make the right decision for your family.

The aforementioned items are the most critical ones that we will review together to determine if the offer submitted fulfills your goals. We will also go through the entire contract in detail, with sellers who are new to the selling process.

Seller's Estimated Net Sheet

I can provide you with an estimated net sheet showing the amount you will net at closing after all costs, based on the offer submitted. This helps you make an informed decision when accepting, or countering offers.

RECEIVING MULTIPLE OFFERS

Receiving multiple offers can be a blessing, but must be handled masterfully. When we receive more than one offer on your home, I will generally contact both agents and let them know that we received multiple offers. Then, I will invite their clients to counter with their highest and best offer. This strategy can sometimes generate offers that are above our list price! However, as I mentioned in Chapter 3, if we accept an offer that is outside the range of what the home will appraise for, then the buyer will have difficulty getting a loan.

I always bear in mind that multiple offers can backfire and send skittish buyers "heading for the hills." I have to treat the situation very professionally and coach the buyer's agents through the process. Don't worry. I'm a deal maker, not a deal breaker! I won't allow the deal to fall flat.

Lowball Offers

It is perfectly normal and common to become emotionally upset when you receive an offer that is far below what you consider to be "acceptable." However my advice is to take a step back and relook at the situation. Don't be upset with the buyer who makes this kind of offer. Instead, be upset with all the people who looked at your home and didn't bother to make an offer. A low offer is simply an invitation to negotiate.

Negotiation Is an Art Form

Negotiation is an art form. When negotiating your deal, I will work to achieve your goals while making the buyer feel that they also got a fair shake.

Sometimes negotiation will involve getting the buyer to see beyond dollars and cents. It is quite possible that the buyer's agent did a poor job of advising their client of your home's true value. For this reason, I will sometimes craft a custom letter reemphasizing your home's features, benefits and upgrades, as well as our pricing strategy, proving that your home is worth what we are asking. This strategy often reignites the fire in the buyer by getting them to see how they will also win by accepting our counteroffer. A proper understanding of the facts helps the buyer to move forward with the home they want, at the price you want.

⑧

CLOSING ON THE SALE

Now that your home is under contract, you can relax a little. Of course there are still a few things that can derail the transaction. At this critical juncture, we remain diligent and will do everything humanly possible to ensure a smooth closing for you.

THE BUYER INSPECTION PROCESS

Once your home is under contract, the buyer will typically order a home inspection. It is the inspector's job to check on the major and minor systems in your home. No matter what condition your home is in, the home inspector will almost always find a list of issues.

Once the buyer receives the home inspection report, they will generally review it with their agent and seek advice. Often, the buyer will seek to have some of the issues on the report addressed. It is important for you to know that you are not contractually obligated to fix anything that is found in the inspection report. At the same time, if the buyer finds issues that they cannot live with and you do not agree to address them, the buyer may terminate the transaction.

If we do receive an amendment requesting additional repairs, we will call you to discuss your options and guide you in the decision making process. Generally speaking, you can either 1) agree to fix some or all of the items, 2) agree to provide a *cash allowance* so that the buyer can address these issues after closing, or 3) decide not to provide anything at all.

I always advise my clients to mentally set aside 1% of the sale price to address any repairs that come up during the option period. For example, if your home's price is $315,000, count on about $3,000 set aside (payable at closing) for inspection related issues just in case. Although I will diligently negotiate and seek to minimize your expenses, I don't recommend we sink the deal over this. This is a very emotional time for the buyer. They are about to make the biggest purchase of their life. Minor repair issues can easily be blown out of proportion if not addressed in a way that will satisfy the buyer.

On the other hand, if you had a pre-inspection completed on your property before we put it on the market, you will be much further along and will not be "blindsided" during this process. You will know exactly what the issues are with your home, and I will market your home as one of my "pre-inspected" properties (similar to a certified pre-owned luxury car).

Because I employ a wide variety of negotiation techniques, I hardly ever have a property fall out of contract. Unless the buyer is being extremely unreasonable and will not relent, we will be able to reach an amicable resolution to most inspection related issues.

CONTRACT TO CLOSE

I utilize a highly efficient closing system that has a proven track record. Rest assured that all of the closing details will be handled on your behalf.

OUT OF TOWN SELLERS

Whether you are traveling at the time of your closing or have already relocated, it's important for you to know that you can close your transaction from anywhere in the United States. The escrow company can either set you up with a mobile notary or they will send the closing packet to you and you can have the documents signed in front of a notary. Many banks provide notary services at no charge.

THE DAY OF CLOSING

Allow yourself about one hour to sign the closing documents. The company closing escrow will be in constant contact with you during the 48 hours prior to closing and keep you posted on the status. Sometimes the closing time or day can be delayed if the buyer's lender does not provide the closing documents to the title company in time. We will provide you the up-to-the-minute information on where we stand with the closing time so you will never be in the dark.

What to Bring to Closing

- ☐ Wiring Instructions — bring a blank check, so that the closing proceeds can be wired to your bank account. You can also opt to receive a check once the transaction funds.
- ☐ Your valid State ID (driver's license or US Passport)
- ☐ Any additional house keys
- ☐ Any additional homeowners manuals (dishwasher, stove, garage door opener, sprinkler system, etc.)
- ☐ Garage door openers
- ☐ Mailbox keys

MY MOVING CHECKLIST

TWO MONTHS BEFORE

- ☐ Collect cartons, gather moving supplies.
- ☐ Select mover and go over all details of the move.
- ☐ Begin packing unnecessary items.
- ☐ Have a yard sale or donate items to a charity.
- ☐ Plan menus to use up food in the cupboards.
- ☐ Contact IRS or your accountant regarding tax deductible expenses.

ONE MONTH BEFORE

- ☐ Begin packing.
- ☐ Notify post office of change of address.
- ☐ Notify utility companies of changes or disconnections.
- ☐ Notify newspaper of address change or discontinuation.
- ☐ Collect and keep important papers handy (medical, etc.)
- ☐ Save moving receipts.
- ☐ Make any reservations for lodging.

- ☐ List important new phone numbers.
- ☐ If employer helps pay moving expenses, confirm what preparations, if any, you will be required to make.
- ☐ Decide what goes with you, what to sell and what to give away.
- ☐ Hold a garage sale or donate items.
- ☐ Finalize arrangements with your moving company, or make reservations if you're renting a truck.
- ☐ Call friends and relatives to let them know when and where you're moving (and to recruit moving day help if needed).

TWO WEEKS BEFORE

- ☐ Clear up outstanding accounts.
- ☐ Transfer checking and savings accounts and contents of safe deposit box.
- ☐ Cancel any direct deposit or automatic payment arrangements on bank account that will be closed.
- ☐ Call the telephone company for assistance in arranging telephone service for your new home.
- ☐ Arrange for pet travel.
- ☐ Return/retrieve borrowed items.
- ☐ Service your car, especially if traveling a distance.
- ☐ Dispose of flammable liquids such as spray paints, aerosols, solvents and thinners; also, gas in yard equipment such as lawn mowers.

- ☐ If shipping a car, empty gas tank to less than ¼ of a tank by move day. Do not completely empty, as mover needs to be able to drive the auto on and off the van.
- ☐ Renew or transfer prescriptions.

WEEK OF MOVE

- ☐ Transfer or close bank account.
- ☐ Defrost refrigerator.
- ☐ Tag furniture to identify its location in the new home.
- ☐ Prepare "survival" package so the family can get along if the moving company is late.
- ☐ Arrange for new cell phone service.

DAY BEFORE MOVE

- ☐ Set aside moving materials, like tape measure, pocket knife, rope, etc.
- ☐ Pick up rental truck if not using a moving company.
- ☐ Check oil and gas in your car.
- ☐ Get a good night's rest.

CONCLUSION...

I want to thank you for investing the time to educate yourself on the home selling process. Selling your home is a life event, and will likely be your single largest transaction representing your biggest asset. Your commitment to educating yourself on the process is wise and I commend you for it.

In this guide we took a poignant look at the following:

1. In chapter 1, we examined the emotional process involved in selling. It can take a toll on you, and preparing yourself mentally is the best strategy.
2. In chapter 2, we looked at what it takes to successfully market your home and the extensive marketing plan I use to successfully market and get your home SOLD.
3. In chapters 3 and 4, we looked at the broad range of information involved in pricing your home and my best tips for getting your home ready for sale.
4. In chapter 5, we looked at how to hire the right agent and net the most money in the least amount of time.

5. In chapters 6–8, I shared my best practices for how to handle showings, work with an offer and get your home successfully closed and SOLD!

If you have any real estate related questions, or wish to set up a free consultation, please contact me.

ABOUT BRENTON FERNANDEZ

Brenton Fernandez' success stems from a result of hard work, consistency and relationship building. He first entered Southern California's real estate market in 1998 investing in rentals and helping others do the same. After moving to Arizona in 2004, he quickly became recognized as the "go to guy" from California renovating and flipping homes making real estate his full-time profession. Nearly 20 years later, Brenton's mission remains the same: to create the very best home buying and selling experience for his clients.

His passion for helping clients sell their home quickly and for top dollar is the very reason his firm was named the #1 brokerage in the East Valley. Trained and developed by Brenton himself, his full-time team is equipped to handle all aspects of the home selling process, and is consistently ranked among the top producing real estate teams in Arizona each and every year. Brenton attributes this accomplishment to some key factors: continuously striving for 110% client satisfaction, and designing his own model to mass market the properties he represents. Going above and beyond traditional real estate methods has translated into over 50% repeat business from past clients and client referrals.

An avid outdoors and sports enthusiast, Brenton finds solace from his day-to-day through long distance running, early morning circuit training at the gym, and fishing with his son. To satisfy his creative side, Brenton redesigns at least five renovation projects each year. Being his own boss in a thriving real estate market also allows him the flexibility to spend time with his three proudest supporters: his wife Erin, son Jack, and newest addition to the family, his daughter Faye.

NOTES:

NOTES:

NOTES:

Made in the USA
Monee, IL
04 November 2026

67385958R10049